JAY-Z

A SHORT UNAUTHORIZED BIOGRAPHY

FAMELIFE BIOS

1

WHO IS JAY-Z

Jay-Z is a famous American rapper, songwriter, music producer, and businessman. Hailed as the King of America by Rolling Stones magazine, Jay-Z is also a seventeen-time Grammy winner. As an artist, he wears many hats in the music industry. From being a rapper, artist, entertainer, and songwriter, he is also a known record producer. Because of his contributions, he is often regarded as one of the most successful men in music.

They were born as Shawn Corey Carter on December 4, 1969, in New York City to parents Adnis Reeves and Gloria Carter. Jay-Z is the youngest of their four children. Having been abandoned by their father, Jay-Z's mother cared for the children independently. They were raised in Marcy Houses or Marcy, a public housing complex in Bedford-Stuyvesant in Brooklyn.

A boom box that was a birthday gift from her mother started Jay-Z's interest in music. Surrounded by drugs, violence, and poverty, music was his saving grace and his escape from all the bad things that were happening all around him. Armed with his boombox, he started rhyming and freestyling under the mentorship of Jonathan Burks or more commonly known as Jaz-O, an 80s rapper and record producer. The budding rapper was known as Jazzy in the neighborhood, but he adopted the name Jay-Z in tribute to his mentor. Jay-Z can be heard in some tracks in Jaz-O's 80s and 90s recordings. Jay-Z started joining rap battles in the early 90s. Some of his early struggles are against LL Cool J, who would be a big name in the industry as well. He was affiliated with more prominent names before he released *In My Life*, his first official rap single with an accompanying music video that he released in 1995. The rapper sold CDs out of his car, and in 1995 he founded Roc-A-Fella Records, an independent label, with other rappers including Kareem "Biggs" Burke and Damon "Dame" Dash. The year after Jay-Z released his debut album, *Reasonable Doubt,* under a distribution deal with Priority which received positive reviews. This would be just the start of Jay-Z's prosperous music career.

Jay-Z wasn't just able to bring his career up out of nothing. Later on, he also cultivated the careers of future big stars Rihanna, Kanye West, and Ne-Yo. After his album The *Black Album* was released in 2003, he sat as the president of Def Jam Recordings, only to resign four years later in 2007. In 2015, Jay-Z and several high-powered friends launched Tidal, a streaming music service. In 2018, Jay-Z and his wife, superstar Beyonce, started their On The Run II Tour in Cardiff in the UK, and ten days later, they released *Everything is Love*, the husband and wife studio album under the name *The Carters*. From his humble beginnings in Brooklyn to the world stage, Jay-Z has proven that if you work hard enough for what you want, the universe will conspire to help you achieve it.

THINGS PEOPLE HAVE SAID ABOUT JAY-Z

Jay-Z and his family may not have had the best life growing up, but there's no denying that his mother, Gloria Carter, cared for and loved him and his three older siblings dearly. According to his mother, she knew Jay-Z was special because among all her children, the famous rapper was her last kid, and he was the only one who did not make her suffer when she was pregnant with him.

Jay-Z is often regarded as one of the greatest rappers in the world. In an article written by Tino Chibbe for the website, Medium, he stated that Jay-Z excels in all the most essential areas that rappers should be good at. These include Flow, Rhyme, Voice, Delivery, Wordplay, and Subject Matter. His bars are also commendable. As a songwriter, Jay-Z can come up with clever lyrics. Chibbe also described Jay-Z to be the archetype of a successful rapper.

JAY-Z IS BORN

Shawn Corey Carter was born on December 4, 1969, in Brooklyn. He was raised in the drug-infested neighborhood in Marcy Houses in Bedford-Stuyvesant. His father was Adnis Reeves, and his mother was Gloria Carter. He is the youngest of four children: Michelle (or Mickey), Andre (or Annie), three older siblings, and Eric. Having been abandoned by her husband, Gloria raised the kids independently.

The rapper's mother, Gloria Carter, grew up on the East Coast. She also lived in a housing project in New York, much like Marcy Houses. 11 years after Jay-Z was born, her husband left the whole family, and Gloria had to raise the kids on her own. Gloria said that she used to take an extra job as a security personnel to provide for the family. Jay-Z described his childhood as hard as they would experience the gas going off or bills not being paid, but they weren't starving. Her mother had made sure that her kids were eating and that everyone was okay.

Adnis Reeves, on the other hand, didn't have much connection with his kids when he went away. Jay-Z had reportedly cut him out of his life. But in 2003, Reeves suffered from liver failure. Gloria urged her son to talk to his father. The two met and eventually reconciled. Jay-Z could forgive his father before he died on June 19, 2003, three months after the reconciliation.

The whole Carter family is American by nationality. They are all ethnic African-American as well.

GROWING UP WITH JAY-Z

J ay-Z grew up in the Marcy Houses in Brooklyn, New York. By all accounts, it's not a friendly environment to raise a family. The neighborhood is drug and gang-infested. But the family had to stay there as only Gloria was working to make ends meet. Jay-Z cut off his father for most of his life, but before his father's demise in 2003, the two reconciled and patched things up. By all accounts, the rapper and her mother have a good relationship. In the album *4:4,* Jay-Z included a poem about his mother coming out to him in *Smile.* Jay-Z reportedly cried tears of joy when his mother finally told him that she was a lesbian.

Jay-Z went to Eli Whitney High School as a young student living in Brooklyn. He attended George Westinghouse Career and Technical Education High School in downtown Brooklyn when the school closed. He was classmates with future rappers Christopher George Latore Wallace or The Notorious B.I.G, and Trevor George Smith Jr.

or Bust Rhymes. He then transferred to Trenton Central High School in New Jersey. Jay-Z did not graduate high school nor get a college degree.

Jay-Z had often rapped about his rough childhood in his songs. He had stated in interviews that in his high school days, he sold cocaine and was also a three-victim of gun shooting.

PERSONAL RELATIONSHIPS

With a career like Jay-Z, scandals are always not far behind. He had been linked to multiple women, but his party neither confirmed nor denied these alleged relationships. Before Jay-Z met, fell in love, and married the superstar Beyonce, we were reported to have dated other celebrities.

In 1999, it was reported that Jay-Z dated fellow star Aaliyah. They were said to be the hottest hip-hop couple at the time though Aaliyah was nine years his junior. However, the two were reportedly in a love triangle with Jay-Z's Roc-a-Fella business partner, Damon Dash. Dash was reported to have pursued the singer about the same time Jay-Z did. The couple split up in 2000, and Aaliyah went on to date Dash until her untimely death in 2001 at the young age of 22. Jay-Z was reported to have attended the funeral rights.

Jay-Z was then reported to be dating rapper Charli Baltimore. The two weren't as hot topics as Jay-Z and Aaliyah, but it was rumored that the relationship between the two rappers was severe. So serious that Jay-Z allegedly stabbed music industry exec Lance "Un" Rivera because of Baltimore. At first, the fight was believed to have broken out because River allegedly leaked the 1999 album *Vol. 3.... Life and Times of S. Carter* of the rapper. But in 2016, rapper Cam'Ron stated that the two were arguing over Baltimore.

In 2000, the rapper was allegedly romantically involved with actress and activist Rosario Dawson. There were a lot of speculations, but neither party confirmed nor denied the rumors. Some rumors suggested that the rapper and actress were together for three years until the two reportedly broke up after Jay-Z admitted that he was crushing on Beyonce, who he met in Cancun, Mexico, during the MTV Spring Break Festival. However, both Jay-Z and Beyonce explained the timeline of their relationship, highlighting that Beyonce couldn't be the reason for the split since after Cancun, they only began talking two years later.

Music's power couple decided to start their relationship on the down-low. Jay-Z and Beyonce collaborated on the 2002 song *03 Bonnie and Clyde*. They again collaborated on Beyonce's debut and sophomore album, sparking rumors about their relationship. Even though they were often seen together in events and sports games, the two kept mum about it. The two officially announced their status when they attended the 2004 VMAs, and in an intimate ceremony in 2008, the couple tied the knot in New York City. The two announced that they were expecting in the 2011 MTV VMAs after Beyonce performed her hit song *Love on Top*, and they welcomed their baby girl, Blue Ivy, on January 7, 2012. Amidst all the rumors in the Knowles-Carter family, the couple went on their first collaborative tour, *On the Run,* in

2014. In 2017, the couple announced that they were pregnant with twins on an explosive Instagram post. The couple welcomed Sir and Rumi Carter in June of the same year, completing their family of five. Shortly after, the couple renewed their wedding vows in another secret ceremony, this time with their kids included.

6

THE RISE OF JAY-Z

His mother said that as a child, Jay-Z would often wake up the whole house as he bangs the kitchen table as a makeshift drum kit so, for his birthday, his mother had given him a boom box. This had piqued his music interest early on. With a childhood as rough as his, he quickly turned to rap, freestyling, and writing music to escape all the bad things surrounding him, including violence, drugs, and poverty. He was mentored by 80s rapper and music producer Jaz-O, and Jay-Z can be heard in some of his old records. As a neophyte rapper, Jay-Z would often join rap battles and often appear in other rapper's songs until he released *In My Lifetime*, his first official rap single. As a rapper with no representation, Jay-Z resorted to selling CDs out of his car before founding Roc-A-Fella Records with Damon Dash and Kareem Burke. His first album, *Reasonable Doubt*, distributed by Priority, received positive reviews from critics and reached number 23 on the Billboard 200 chart. He then stroked another distribution deal with Def Jam when he released his sophomore album *In My Life, Vol. 1.* The album chronicled Jay-Z's tough childhood and his sadness caused by the passing of his good friend, rapper Notorious B.I.G. In 1998, the rapper released his third studio album *Vol. 2... Hard Knock Life.* Included in this album was his biggest hit as an up-and-coming rapper, *Hard Knock Life (Ghetto Anthem).* This album is often called his most commercially successful album. The rapper was featured in Mariah Carey's 1999 song *Heart-breaker.* The song stayed at the top of the Hot 100, making it Jay-Z's first chart-topper. Shortly after, Jay-Z released another successful album, *Vol. 3... Life and Times of S. Carter.* He released *The Dynasty: Roc La Familia,* which introduced other newcomers, including The Neptunes, Just Blaze, Bink, and most notably Kanye West. Jay-Z then released the widely successful *The Blueprint* a few hours after the 9/11 terrorist attacks. Eminem was the only rapper featured in the album. He produced and rapped in *Renegade,* and Kanye West was said to have four songs. In 2002, the rapper released his double-album titled *The Blueprint²: The Gift & The Curse* before reissuing a single-disc version called *The Blueprint 2.1* featuring artists including Beyonce, Lenny Kravitz, Faith Evans, Kanye West, and the late The Notorious B.I.G.

At the opening of the 40/40 Club, Jay-Z released *The Black Album,* which featured collaborations with producers including Just Blaze, Kanye West, The Neptunes, Eminem, Timbaland, 9th Wonder, DJ Quick, Rick Rubin, and The Buchanans. He also released his first collaboration album entitled *The Best of Both Worlds* with singer-songwriter R. Kelly. He then staged his "retirement party" at the Madison Square Garden on November 25, 2003, attended by fellow artists and collaborations including The Roots, Memphis

Bleek, Missy Elliot, Freeway, Beanie Siegel, Twista, Beyonce, Ghostface Killax, Pharrell Williams, R. Kelly, and Foxy. Brown. The mothers of late rappers The Notorious B.I.G. and Tupac Shakur were also in attendance. The concert marked Jay-Z's retirement from making and releasing new studio albums. He then focused on side projects and collaborations. He released a most extraordinary hits record and a sophomore collaborative album with R. Kelly entitled *Unfinished Business*. He also worked with Linkin Park in their remix EP called *Collision Course*, and Jay-Z also sat as the executive producer of Fort Minor's debut album, *The Rising Tide*. Towards the end of 2004, Jay-Z became the president of Def Jam Records and Roc-A-Fella Records. However, the move caused a rift between former business partners Damon Dash and Kareem Burke.

In 2005, Jay-Z headlined Powerhouse, Power 105.1's annual concert. Entitled *I Declare War*, concertgoers speculated that Jay-Z would declare war with his enemies in the hip-hop industry. Still, contrary to all speculations, Jay-Z concluded many arguments in the concert. The year after, the rapper released his comeback album *Kingdom Come* and in 2017, the rapper released *American Gangster* inspired by the Ridley Scott film of the same name. In 2008, it was announced that Jay-Z was set to headline Glastonbury Festival making him the first hip-hop artist to be the most significant act in the British music festival. He went on to headline several other music festivals in Europe in 2008. In September 2009, Jay-Z released *The Blueprint 3*, which was his eleventh album, and the month after, the rapper kicked off *The Blueprint 3* tour. In 2009, Jay-Z left Def Jam and started Roc Nation with Live Nation. He also partnered with Stargate to form StarRoc. The rapper also tried producing a theater play entitled *Fela!* with husband and wife duo Jada

Pinkett Smith and Will Smith. In June 2010, Eminem and Jay-Z announced *The Home and Home Tour*, a pair of concerts in New York and Detroit. Jay-Z also went on tour as the support act of U2's Australia and New Zealand concert legs. In 2011, the rapper launched a website called *Life + Times* in a blog-like format covering topics including music, fashion, sports, and technology. It was reported that Jay-Z was very hands-on with the blog.

In 2012, Jay-Z announced to be the headliner for the first-ever *Budweiser Made in America,* a Philadelphia music festival set to be an annual event. The rapper and Rihanna also headlined BBC Radio 1's Hackney Weekend music festival in 2012. In December 2012, Coldplay played alongside Jay-Z in the Barclays Center in Brooklyn. After appearing in Justin Timberlake's song *Suit and Tie*, the two set out to headline *Legends of the Summer Stadium Tour*, and during the 2013 NBA Finals, the rapper announced that he would release *Magna Carta Holy Grail*. His new studio album hit the stores in July 2013. In early June 2017, several posters and internet banner ads appeared teasing a project titled *4:44,* and by mid-June, the project was confirmed to be a new Jay-Z album. The album was released online on July 2, and the physical albums were made available five days after. In June 2018, Jay-Z and Beyonce set out to start their collaborative concert tour, *On the Run II*. At their final performance in London, the two released. *Everything is Love*, a joint studio album credited under the name The Carters.

7

SIGNIFICANT CAREER MILESTONES

No wonder Jay-Z is one of the biggest names in the music industry. He was able to headline and perform in sold-out concerts worldwide, and the albums that he released were all big hits. Every new album was also sure to have a chart-topper. His first album, *Reasonable Doubt,* reached platinum and was named one of the 500 Greatest Albums of All Time by the *Rolling Stones.* His sophomore album *In My Life, Vol. 1* was more of a commercial success than his debut album, which reached platinum in the US. *Vol. 2... Hard Knock Life* included *Hard Knock Life (Ghetto Anthem)* which was arguably his biggest hit song at the time. *Vol. 2* was able to sell over five million copies worldwide and earned 5x platinum in the country. *Vol. 2* was also a Grammy-winning album. *Vol. 3...*

Life and Times of S. Carter were able to sell over three million copies worldwide, and the soulful album *The Dynasty: Roc La Familia* was able to sell two million copies in the U.S. On September 11, 2001, Jay-Z released *The Blueprint,* which debuted at the top of Billboard 200, sold over 427,000 units, and earned 2x platinum in the US. The album was highly regarded for the excellent mix of mainstream and hardcore rap. It's now being preserved in the National Recording Registry after being chosen by the Library of Congress for being significant culturally, aesthetically, and historically. The double album *The Blueprint2: The Gift & The Curse* debuted at the top of Billboard 200 and had sold over 3 million copies in the country. *The Black Album* was a commercial success selling over 3 million units in the country. With Linkin Park, *Numb/Encore* won the Grammy for Best Rap/Song Collaboration.

In 2016, his comeback album *Kingdom Come* sold over 680,000 units on just its first week of release despite its single *Show Me What You Got leakage*. The album was said to be the biggest first-week earner of his whole career, and it went on to sell over two million units in the country. His tenth album, *American Gangster*, sold over one million copies, and his eleventh, *The Blueprint 3*, became his eleventh album to have reached the top on Billboard 200. He's the current record holder of the most albums to have reached number one in the chart. *Watch the Throne debuted* on the top spot on the iTunes Store in twenty-three different countries. It also sold 290,000 copies on the music streaming site. His album, *Magna Carta Holy Grail*, was able to sell over 500,000 units in its first week alone and debuted on the top of Billboard 200. He also earned nine Grammy nominations for the album in 2014. *4:44* received the same welcome, if not better. Sprint bought one million copies of the album, and because of this Recording Industry Association of America (RIAA) awarded *4:44* platinum. The album also debuted at the top of Billboard 200 and earned several Grammy nominations, including Album and Record of the Year.

JAY-Z'S FRIENDS AND FOES

J ay-Z couldn't get to the top without a few feuds on the way. The hip-hop industry is filled with fat bank accounts and closed mouths. It's easy to ruffle some feathers and diss your enemies in your songs. The case was the same with Jay-Z. He had high-profile feuds that took the spotlight other than his artistry.

Most notably is his feud with Nas. In 2001, they spoke out against another rapper, Prodigy, who took offense in a line in the Jay-Z song Money, Cash, Hoes. Jay-Z then performed at Summer Jam in the same year and sang Takeover. While doing so, the rapper revealed photos of Prodigy dressed like the King of Pop, Michael Jackson. Another line in the song was a dig at another rapper, Nas, who criticized Jay-Z on We Will Survive. Nas retaliated with a song called Ether dissing Jay-Z. The rapper quickly added another verse in Takeover to further diss Nas. Jay-Z was also in disagreement with former business partners Damon Dash and Kareem Burke when he sat as the president of Def

Jam Records and decided to take control of the two labels, including Roc-A-Fella, which he founded with his two friends. Noel Gallagher also criticized the committee of the Glastonbury Festival, who chose Jay-Z to headline at the festival. Gallagher and his band *Oasis* was a former headliner at the festival, and he said that Glastonbury has a tradition of playing guitar music. Jay-Z retaliated by singing one of *Oasis'* most famous songs *Wonderwall* when he got on stage before singing *99 Problems*.

Though his names had been dragged through the mud, Jay-Z had stayed friends with a lot of people. He grew up and was friends with the late rapper The Notorious B.I.G and Tupac Shakur. He had even invited his friends' mothers to a concert in the Madison Square Garden. Jay-Z also shares a good relationship with Bono, his band U2, and Bono's wife. He's also good friends with producers including Just Blaze, The Neptunes, and the Buchanans. He also fostered Kanye West's career and West-produced songs for him. Jay-Z is also friends with Eminem, Timbaland, and Justin Timberlake.

FUN FACT ABOUT JAY-Z

You know an artist is significant when the FBI interferes with an issue. The case is the same with Jay-Z. Ahead of *Kingdom Come's* release in 2006, the lead single *Show Me What You Got* was leaked on the internet. The song received heavy air-play that the FBI was called in to investigate. Jay-Z reportedly writes his lyrics in his head and doesn't write any of the words down. The rapper is also Beyonce's go-to person when she records new material to ask for his opinion.

HOW THE WORLD SEES JAY-Z

Jay-Z has proven that he can do everything. He is an award-winning artist, and he is a successful businessman. He is also a husband and a father to his three kids. He had accomplished so much musically, and he is yet to stop. It seems like he's always working on something, whether the project is his or someone else's. The man doesn't give the idea that he's stopping anytime soon.

In 2017, Jay-Z was named Rap's first billionaire. The combined net worth of him and his wife is upwards of one billion dollars. This is due to his albums' sales, endorsement deals, and profits from his businesses, among many others. Jay-Z had dipped his toes in many business ventures from tech to fashion to sports. Jay-Z partnered with Bing on the release of his memoir *Decoded*. The rapper is also an investor in Carol's Daughter's Brooklyn-based beauty brand. He also partnered with Rhapsody, the digital music service and luxury watch brand Hublot. He also starred in a commercial for Hewlett-Packard. Jay-Z is also part of Budweiser's global ad campaign, which aims to build the beer brand's global presence. He also designed a sneaker line for Reebok. Jay-Z's company Roc Nation also has a $20 million deal with Samsung Galaxy. Jay-Z is also an investor in the Brooklyn Nets. He's also an endorser of the champagne brand Armand de Brignac, Cherry Coke, Chrysler, Duracell, D'Usse, and Heineken. He also owns 40/40, Rocawear, and Rocawear Cologne. Jay-Z said in an interview that he's not a businessman. He's the business, man. Truly.

Religion wasn't much of a priority in the Carter household growing up. But according to Jay-Z, living in Brooklyn opened his eyes to many ways of believing. He stated that he believed in one God, but he doesn't believe in religion because religion separated people. He said that with whatever religion, it's the same God. He also added that he doesn't believe in hell. Jay-Z had also distanced himself in politics. In an interview, he said that he has zero interest in politics because he thinks it's a bunch of liars and self-interest. He said he believed in hope and people. But when Obama campaigned for the presidency, Jay-Z was vocal in his support of the presidential hopeful. The Obamas and the Carters are known to be buddies. Jay-Z also supports Obama's Buffet Rule saying that he wouldn't mind paying more taxes if it's sure to go to important things like education and poverty.

Jay-Z is also prominent in supporting charities and causes. In 2006, he met with UN Sec-Gen Kofi Anna. He vowed to raise awareness about the water shortage on his upcoming world tour during the meeting. In the same year, he filmed a documentary entitled *Diary of Jay-Z: Water for Life* chronicling his events in Africa when he visited. When

Hurricane Katrina came, he donated one million dollars for the American Red Cross to help the tragedy victims. His 2006 concert in New York City was also able to raise over 250,00 thousand dollars to be donated to PlayPumps International. He is also a supporter of Artists for Peace and Justice, Broadway Cares/Equity Fights AIDS, Boys & Girls Clubs of America, GLAAD, Global Poverty Project, Global Citizen, and the GRAMMY Foundation. He also supports Keep A Child Alive, Music for Relief, Multiple Myeloma Research Foundation, United Way, and Robin Hood. Together with his mother, Gloria, the rapper founded The Shawn Carter Foundation, which aims to help eligible students with socio-economic problems to finish college. It was also revealed by the co-author of his memoir that Jay-Z set up a trust fund for the children of Sean Bell, who was shot by the police the morning before his wedding. Jay-Z had also bailed out protesters during protests against police brutality. Jay-Z and their wife Beyonce have also been active supporters of the Black Lives Matter movement, even donating 1.5 million dollars to the different social justice groups. The rapper also bought advertising space in newspapers nationwide, including The New York Times, The Chicago Tribune, The Atlanta Journal-Constitution, and The Los Angeles Times to honor police brutality victim George Floyd.

Jay-Z has come a long way. From his rough childhood in Brooklyn to his mansion in Los Angeles, he had achieved all that he had hoped for and more. He was also strong enough to fight for important causes. He continues to be a pillar of the hip-hop industry and all of the music hopefuls in the world. He had started as an independent artist selling CDs out of his car, and now he is at the top of the food chain.

He's been through a lot, and he has always been honest with his stories. He's loved worldwide not only for his songs and his albums but also for the inspiration that he gives to young people about achieving their dreams.

11

Sources:

Https://medium.com/@Tino_X_O/rap-rushmore-the-4-greatest-rappers-of-all-time-jay-z-cc4948b216d

https://www.mamamia.com.au/who-is-jay-zs-mum/

https://peoplepill.com/people/adnes-reeves/

https://www.nme.com/news/music/jay-z-mother-gloria-carter-moving-speech-coming-out-2309826

https://www.cheatsheet.com/entertainment/aaliyah-and-2-other-celebrities-you-forgot-jay-z-reportedly-dated.html/

https://theblast.com/132822/timeline-of-jay-z-rosario-dawsons-previous-love-story-what-went-

https://www.businessinsider.com/jay-zs-product-endorsement-deals-2013-7

https://www.vulture.com/2013/07/complete-list-of-every-product-endorsed-by-jay-z.html

https://hollowverse.com/jay-z/

https://www.looktothestars.org/celebrity/jay-z

https://www.independent.co.uk/arts-entertainment/music/news/jay-z-blackout-tuesday-advert-george-floyd-black-lives-matter-a9548941.html

https://en.wikipedia.org/wiki/Jay-Z#Personal_life

Photo Credit

J ay-Z in Hamburg/Germany 2003
19 March 2003
Mikamote [CC BY-SA 3.0 (https://creativecom-
mons.org/licenses/by-sa/3.0)]

Jay-Z at a concert in 2006
21 October 2006
i am guilty [CC BY-SA 2.0 (https://creativecommon-
s.org/licenses/by-sa/2.0)]

Shawn 'Jay-Z' Carter Foundation Carnival Hudson River
Park; Pier 54 September 29th 2011 New York City
29 September 2011
Joella Marano from Manhattan, NY [CC BY-SA 2.0
(https://creativecommons.org/licenses/by-sa/2.0)]

Shawn 'Jay-Z' Carter Foundation Carnival 2011
29 September 2011
Joella Marano [CC BY-SA 2.0 (https://creativecommon-
s.org/licenses/by-sa/2.0)]

Shawn 'Jay-Z' Carter Foundation Carnival Hudson River Park; Pier 54 September 29th 2011 New York City

24 February 2013

Printed in Dunstable, United Kingdom